Digital Assets
Unravel the Secrets of Web-Based Wealth Creation

Table of Contents

Chapter 1. Introduction

Welcome to an enlightening journey that explores the marvels of this digital era, riding on the waves of the Internet revolution. Our Special Report, "Digital Assets: Unravel the Secrets of Web-Based Wealth Creation" demystifies the complex landscape of online investing, shining a light on the labyrinth of digital assets in a way that's engaging and approachable. Whether you're a newcomer or a seasoned investor, this comprehensive study will equip you with the tools and knowledge you need to navigate the booming world of web-based assets with intelligence and finance acumen. With real-world examples, expert insights, and step-by-step guidance, you will learn to leverage existing technology and capitalise on future trends. Be prepared to unlock untold riches hidden within the digital world and elevate your financial game to new heights!

Chapter 2. Understanding Digital Assets: An Introduction

In the twinkling binaries of the cyber universe lurks a universe of opportunities, unseen by most, yet, profusely enriching to those who dare to voyage amidst its myriad digital constellations. This elusive world is also known as the realm of digital assets. A term often shrouded in mystery and misperceptions, digital assets have the potential to redefine economies and the way we perceive investments today.

2.1. Defining Digital Assets

Simply put, a digital asset refers to any information stored in a binary format, that comes with the right to use. These data files are distinguished from traditional assets based on their binary composition, their ability to be stored, transmitted electronically, and stem from the major advancements in computer science and technology.

The universe of digital assets is far from being confined to just cryptocurrencies and non-fungible tokens (NFTs), it is a vast expanse inhabited by a plethora of innate and intricate components. Website domains, digital currencies, patents, copyrights, electronic databases, software and digital media like photos, music, and videos, etc. form integral parts of this digital assets universe.

2.2. Diving Into the Classification of Digital Assets

To navigate this expansive universe, it's essential to begin by understanding the types and classifications of digital assets.

1. **Cryptocurrencies**: Predominantly referred to as digital currencies, they make use of cryptography techniques for secure, peer-to-peer transactions that take place over the internet. Bitcoin, Ethereum, and Ripple are prime examples.

2. **Utility Tokens**: Apart from facilitating digital cash transactions, these tokens provide users with a product or service. For instance, Ethereum's Ether token provides access to its platform's functionalities.

3. **Non-Fungible Tokens (NFTs)**: These digital signatures stored on blockchain technology assure unique attributes and authenticity of an item, guaranteeing its value.

4. **Security Tokens**: Regulated digital contracts that represent the ownership information of the real-world asset, security tokens can include shares in a company, interest in a fund or a trust, or real estate.

5. **Digital Intellectual Property**: This includes website domains, patents, copyrights, software, and databases.

The availability of these varied digital assets have changed the complexion of modern day investment horizons, transforming methods in which wealth is accumulated and stored.

2.3. From Traditional to Digital: A Crucial Paradigm Shift

Performing a correlatory analysis between digital and traditional assets goes a long way in facilitating an understanding of this new economic wave. Like their physical counterparts, digital assets add value to their holder or creator, can be bought, sold, owned, and have a measurable life span.

But in contrast to traditional assets, digital assets typically generate value through utility and scarcity, rather than tangible physical form. Their prices are often driven by speculative investments and the perceived future utility of the asset, thus, volatility is a key feature in digital asset markets.

2.4. Echoes of Digital Risks and Rewards

With reward, comes risk, however, digital assets are not the exception to this timeless rule. They share some common risks with traditional investments, such as market risk due to fluctuating prices. Yet, digital assets can pose unique risks including cybersecurity threats, regulatory uncertainties, lack of recourse if lost or stolen, reliance on technology infrastructure and potential margin pressures.

Despite the risks, digital assets' potential for high returns and the unique opportunities they offer for diversification has made them a fixture in many investment portfolios.

2.5. Panoramic View of the Digital Ecosystem

The digital ecosystem encapsulates an array of stakeholders, each playing a critical role in the mechanisms of the digital asset marketplace. These stakeholders include developers, users, investors, miners, validators, exchanges, wallets, and regulators.

Understanding these key players and their roles is crucial in grasping the intricacies of digital asset investments.

2.6. Retraceable Steps: History and Evolution

The history of digital assets can be traced back to the birth of Bitcoin in 2009. Ever since, this space has witnessed a series of evolutionary leaps, heralding new forms of digital assets. Understanding this timeline not just offers an enriching perspective on how far we have come, but also delivers a speculative glimpse into a technologically transcendent future.

2.7. The Tomorrow of Digital Assets: Future Trends

All signs point to the continued development and expansion of the digital asset universe. Future trends include tokenisation of tangible assets, development of decentralised finance (DeFi), and increasing regulatory clarity.

Thus, when traversing the tracks of the digital express, an understanding of digital assets is but a ticket, opening up portals to newer realms of wealth accumulation. Unmasking these intricacies helps one shape a cogent financial strategy, thereby aiding wealth creation and upscaling one's investment acumen.

Chapter 3. Beyond Bitcoin: A Broader Universe of Cryptocurrencies

In the realm of online investing, cryptocurrencies have long emerged from the shadow of obscurity. As stakeholders of the internet revolution, we've grown familiar with Bitcoin, the pioneer in this field. But, beyond the buzz surrounding Bitcoin, there thrives a much broader universe of cryptocurrencies that promises exciting investment opportunities and revolutionary financial dynamics.

3.1. Breaking Down Cryptocurrencies

Cryptocurrencies are digital or virtual currencies that utilize cryptography for security. They function on as decentralised networks based on blockchain technology - a distributed ledger enforced by a network of computers or 'nodes'. This complex world of digital currencies suggests an impending shift away from traditional forms of wealth and toward this innovative concept of 'money'.

Since the launch of Bitcoin in 2009, the cryptocurrency landscape has exploded with a wealth of digital assets, each bearing unique characteristics and promising significant value. Discovering these alternatives might seem like navigating a labyrinth, but knowledge is your compass.

3.2. Alternative Coins or 'Altcoins'

Post the introduction of Bitcoin, most other cryptocurrencies were introduced as variants and have been aptly named as 'Altcoins', short for alternative coins. Often designed using the basic framework provided by Bitcoin, these digital currencies introduce changes to address perceived limitations or to provide novel features. Some well-known altcoins include Ethereum, Ripple (XRP), Litecoin, and Monero.

Ethereum was introduced in 2015 and is currently the second-largest cryptocurrency by market cap after Bitcoin. Unlike Bitcoin, Ethereum's focus extends beyond the role of a digital currency. It features 'smart contracts' that are self-executing with the terms of the agreement directly written into the code. This allows for programmable money and has facilitated the creation of decentralized finance (DeFi) applications and non-fungible tokens (NFTs).

Ripple (XRP) is aimed at improving international money transfers. By connecting banks and payment providers, Ripple provides a seamless experience to transfer money globally. XRP is the digital asset that facilitates transactions on the Ripple Network, speeding up the process and making it more secure.

Litecoin, introduced in 2011, was an early Bitcoin spinoff or 'fork'. It offers quicker transaction confirmation times and a different hash algorithm.

Monero stands out for its emphasis on privacy. It obscures the sender, recipient, and amount of every transaction. This commitment to privacy makes Monero more fungible and discourages censorship of its transactions.

3.3. Tokenization

Other types of digital assets are the so-called 'tokens,' which are generally built on top of another blockchain, like Ethereum's. Tokens can represent virtually anything that's fungible and tradable, from commodities to loyalty points to even other cryptocurrencies. Creating tokens is a much easier process as you do not have to modify the codes from a particular protocol or create a blockchain from scratch. All you have to do is follow a standard template on the blockchain–like on the Ethereum platform–that allows you to create your own tokens.

Tokens have pushed the boundaries of what can be traded and owned. They've facilitated novel economic systems, such as the increasingly popular Decentralized Finance (DeFi) and innovative avenues for artists and content creators, like Non-Fungible Tokens (NFTs).

DeFi leverages blockchain technology to decentralize traditional financial systems. By cutting out the middleman, DeFi offers a range of financial activities–from loans and insurance to trading, savings, and more–directly between participants.

Non-Fungible Tokens (NFTs) offer unique cryptographic tokens with each unique token representing a unique digital asset. This uniqueness and scarcity are what give them value. NFTs have surged in popularity, particularly within the art world, offering digital artists the opportunity to sell their work in a way that provides proof of authenticity and ownership to buyers.

3.4. The Technology Behind Cryptocurrencies

An understanding of the technology that powers cryptocurrencies is crucial for any investor. The two most vital components of this technology are cryptographic hash functions and blockchain.

A cryptographic hash function is a special class of hash function that has certain properties which make it ideal for cryptography. It is a mathematical operation that takes an input - or 'message' - and returns a fixed-size string of bytes, which appears random to those who do not know the secret. This function is deterministic, meaning the same input will always produce the same output–an essential feature for tracking transactions and balances on the blockchain.

The blockchain is a revolutionary technology enabling transfer of digital assets without the need for an intermediary. In essence, it is a chain of blocks, where each block records information about transactions. The transparency, immutability, and security provided by the blockchain make it an ideal platform for the transfer and storage of value.

3.5. Assessing your Cryptocurrency Investments

Investing in cryptocurrencies should not be approached on a whim. Similar to normal investing, you should evaluate the purpose, potential use case, technological complexity, and the team behind the cryptocurrency.

Understanding the purpose and use case of the cryptocurrency is essential. Each token serves a different purpose. Some tokens might represent a share in a company, some offer access to a service, while others might function as a currency.

Evaluating the technology behind a coin can be challenging given the complex nature of this field. It might require a basic understanding of blockchain principles and how they're applied. However, the main goal should be to assess whether the technology is solving a real problem or is it just a solution looking for a problem.

It's also important to consider the team who is behind the cryptocurrency. Researching who is on the team, their past experiences, whether they've been involved in other cryptocurrencies before, and if so, how successful were they are critical factors for potential investment.

As with any investment, cryptocurrencies come with their own set of risks. Their largely unregulated and volatile nature means that investors should be prepared for the possibility of large price swings.

In conclusion, the world beyond Bitcoin is vast and full of exciting investment opportunities. However, they require a comprehensive understanding and careful consideration. By investing the time and effort to understand this diverse landscape, investors can position themselves to take a meaningful part in this digital revolution, potentially reaping high rewards.

Chapter 4. Digital Tokens and ICOs: The New Frontier of Fundraising

Today's financial landscape is experiencing a remarkable shift through the widespread use of blockchain technology, reshaping traditional methods of fundraising, trading, and transactions. Digital tokens and Initial Coin Offerings (ICOs) sit at the vanguard of this frontier, heralding a new era of investment opportunities and ways to raise capital.

4.1. Understanding Digital Tokens

Digital tokens, often interchangeably termed cryptocurrencies, are unique, virtual tokens predicated on cryptographic technology and can represent a myriad of tangible or intangible assets. Denoting predefined values, they can serve as a medium of exchange, posing a novel alternative to traditional forms of currency. Furthermore, they provide a secure environment, harnessing the power of blockchain to facilitate instant, immutable transactions.

The universe of digital tokens is expansive and encompasses a few broad categories:

- Utility Tokens: These are digital tokens that provide users with future access to a product or service.
- Security Tokens: These are tokens tied to a business, promising future profits or shares.
- Asset Tokens: These represent ownership or stake in a particular asset, like real estate or commodities.

These diverse forms of tokens have spurred an era of digitised assets and investments, acting as pillars of the modern, digital financial ecosystem.

4.2. Initial Coin Offerings (ICOs)

ICOs serve as novel methods for blockchain-based startups to raise funds by selling their tokens to early backers, often before a full-fledged product or service rollout. This prevalent form of fundraising has gained traction, disrupting traditional routes of raising capital.

An ICO process typically involves the creation of a whitepaper detailing the project's objectives, the tokens' specifics, and how the funds raised will be used. Following this, a smart contract is deployed onto the blockchain, stipulating terms for the ICO.

The tokens offered are usually utility tokens, providing early backers with access to the service or product that the startup plans to offer. In some cases, they can also be security tokens, providing investors with an expected future return on investment.

4.3. The Rise and Role of ICOs

Even though ICOs have been relatively recent phenomena, their growth has been exponential. The combination of low barriers to entry, potential high returns, and the exponential increase in blockchain projects have made ICOs a preferred method of fundraising.

ICOs have facilitated the democratization of financing, allowing anyone with internet access to invest in and support projects that resonate with their interests. They've also succeeded in lowering geographical constraints, opening up global opportunities previously limited to specific regions or individuals.

On the flip side, the explosive rise of ICOs has also seen a wave of fraudulent schemes, making it equally important for investors to be vigilant about where and how they invest.

4.4. Conducting Due Diligence on ICOs

Understanding and evaluating an ICO before diving into an investment is crucial. Meticulous due diligence should be considered, examining the project's development team, the whitepaper's credibility, and the project's transparency. ICO rating websites can also provide valuable insights, although investors are advised to cross-verify the information from multiple sources.

The future success of an ICO is inevitably tied to the completion and success of the project it undertakes. Therefore, having a clear and coherent roadmap, coupled with a competent development team, is a strong indicator of the project's credibility.

4.5. Risks Associated with Digital Tokens and ICOs

Investing in digital tokens and ICOs comes with its fair share of risks. Firstly, there is no guarantee that the tokens purchased in an ICO will surge in value. The value may plummet due to several reasons, including the project's failure, scams, or a decrease in token demand.

Regulatory risks also pose significant threats. Countries worldwide are trying to keep up with these new forms of fundraising, with regulation varying significantly from region to region. ICOs banned in specific jurisdictions, or stricter regulations, may dramatically impact the value and viability of tokens.

Lastly, digital tokens are susceptible to cyber attacks. Despite blockchain's secure nature, hackers continuously work on ways to exploit possible vulnerabilities.

4.6. Carving Out the Future of Fundraising

Despite these risks, the benefits and potential of ICOs and digital tokens promise a brave, new world of fundraising and investment. They have ignited a global disruption to traditional financial systems, democratising access to capital and investment opportunities.

As blockchain becomes more accepted and evolves further, we can anticipate a refined regulatory landscape that assures greater transparency, reduces fraud, and protects investor interests. Even as the world faces these profound shifts towards digital assets, it's essential to approach them with a fusion of excitement, scepticism, and informed discernment.

Remember, the world of digital tokens and ICOs is not just about playing the game; it's about understanding the rules, knowing when to play, and when to watch from the sidelines.

Chapter 5. Web 3.0 and The Future of Digital Wealth Creation

The period of Web 3.0 marks the advent of an intelligent, semantically woven web ecosystem that introduces concepts such as interconnectivity, data portability and semantic web technologies. Web 3.0 sees its influence extending to the world of digital assets, as these technologies lay the foundation for an innovative wealth creation ecosystem.

5.1. Understanding the Semantics of Web 3.0

Web 3.0, frequently referred to as the 'semantic web', significantly shifts the internet's paradigm from a widespread collection of information to a structured environment where data is connected, meaningful and readily available for users. The semantic web ties into the concept of data portability and interconnectivity, where information is freely shared between different platforms without compromising its quality or meaning.

Crucial to Web 3.0 is the notion of linked data, where diverse datasets are interconnected to build context around information. Not only does this enable more potent search capabilities, but it also opens the door for machines to comprehend and interact with data independently.

5.2. Portability and Interconnectivity in Digital Wealth Creation

As digital assets become prevalent, the present internet paradigm struggles with issues like data privacy, security, monopolization of data, and interoperability. The significance of Web 3.0 lies in its potential to resolve these challenges. Web 3.0 digital assets could be instantly transferred across numerous platforms, attaining a new degree of liquidity that boosts their value and usability. The ability for digital assets to interact and transact with one another effectively across various ecosystems could lead to new wealth-creation opportunities.

5.3. The Rise of Decentralization and Blockchain

Web 3.0 also gives rise to the concept of decentralized networks. Blockchain, being a prominent example, is not controlled by any central authority and ensures data protection, transparency and integrity. Given their un-centralized nature, blockchain networks deliver a degree of trust and security that is often absent in the age of Web 2.0.

Blockchain has the potential to redefine digital wealth creation. Combining blockchain's public ledger with decentralized finance (DeFi) systems provides a potentially limitless field of digital finance opportunities. DeFi systems disintermediate traditional processes to reduce costs while increasing the efficiency, such as peer-to-peer lending or decentralized exchanges.

5.4. Cryptocurrencies, NFTs and Beyond

Blockchain technology has given birth to cryptocurrencies like Bitcoin and Ethereum, which have not only become an asset class of their own but also ignited the current widespread interest in digital assets. However, cryptocurrencies are only the tip of the iceberg.

Non-fungible tokens (NFTs), a form of digital asset that represents ownership of unique items or content, are gaining popularity. NFTs have started to create a considerable impact in areas such as art, music, and real estate, offering novel avenues for digital wealth creation. The value and influence of such digital asset forms will no doubt escalate in the future Web 3.0 ecosystem.

5.5. Investing in the Web 3.0 Ecosystem

With the evolution of digital assets, investment models have evolved too. Crowdfunding platforms, initial coin offerings (ICOs), and security token offerings (STOs) have emerged as innovative investment pathways. ICOs and STOs leverage the power of blockchain, creating opportunities for individuals to invest in projects at their inception.

In the Web 3.0 environment, digital asset investments will likely be less opaque, more diverse and inclusive. Investing won't be limited to large institutions or the wealthy, but virtually anyone could participate in the initial funding of a promising start-up or a groundbreaking digital art project.

Investors need to understand and adapt to these trends in digital wealth creation to stay relevant. They should be prepared to broaden their portfolio to include more than just traditional asset classes, and possibly engage in more participatory forms of investment.

5.6. Looking Ahead: The Potential of Web 3.0 and Digital Wealth Creation

The narrative of wealth creation in the age of Web 3.0 is only just beginning to unfold. As we progress further into the future, digital assets will continue to grow both in terms of value and diversity. The nature of investments will grow more complex, requiring a more sophisticated understanding of the digital asset marketplace.

The transformative power of Web 3.0 can't be overstated. Web 3.0 and digital assets will continue to evolve, and the new semantic web's potential to redefine our relationship with online data and assets is astonishing.

In this evolving landscape of Web 3.0 and digital assets, it is crucial to understand the fundamental shifts on the horizon and adapt to them. The investors who are willing to look beyond the traditional boundaries, adapt, and evolve stand to foster and unlock a future of unprecedented prosperity.

Web 3.0 promises to be an exciting phase in the digital sphere, heralding an era of vast investment prospects and more equitable, transparent, and efficient modes of wealth creation. Whether one is a digital native or a traditional investor looking to dip their toes into the world of digital assets, the future of digital wealth creation in Web 3.0 offers endless possibilities and opportunities. Welcome to the future.

Chapter 6. NFTs: Digital Artwork as an Asset Class

If you were recently introduced to the concept of 'cryptocurrencies' or 'blockchain,' it's likely that you've also heard of 'Non-Fungible Tokens' or 'NFTs.' These are making headlines for the massive sums they're fetching at auctions, while also challenging traditional notions regarding art, its ownership, and the value of digital belongings.

We begin our journey by defining these digital novelties to level the playing field for a deeper dive into their implications.

6.1. What are Non-Fungible Tokens?

Non-Fungible Tokens, or NFTs, are cryptographic assets on blockchain with unique identification codes and metadata that distinguish them from each other. Unlike cryptocurrencies like Bitcoin or Ethereum that are fungible and can be exchanged on a like-for-like basis, NFTs aren't interchangeable.

This distinctive quality comes from the use of smart contracts, self-executing contracts with the terms of the agreement directly written into code, which adds information or attributes that make these tokens unique. These attributes could include anything from ownership details to digital artwork, effectively certifying a digital file's authenticity and ownership.

6.2. NFTs and the Art World

In the art world, NFTs serve as a digital certificate of ownership linked to a piece of art, which could include music, video, or other forms of creative work. NFTs have provided a platform for digital artists to sell their works for a handsome profit, which was unimaginable a few years ago.

The success story of artist Mike Winkelmann, better known as Beeple, has pushed NFTs into the limelight. He sold his artwork for a whopping $69 million, instantly becoming one of the top three most valuable living artists. This example is a demonstration of the potential value of digital artwork, which was previously often overlooked or undervalued in traditional markets.

6.3. Evaluating NFTs as an Asset

For investors, NFTs offer a new asset class that could potentially yield high returns. While their popularity is relatively recent, their potential implications can't be overlooked. Rapid price appreciation, especially in arts, games, and other collectibles linked to NFTs, indicate the possibility of high yield investments.

However, like any investment, NFTs also come with risk. Their value, similar to most art and collectibles, is highly subjective and depends largely on the perceptions of collectors or investors. Their prices can fluctuate widely and unpredictability is a common trait.

6.4. Collecting Digital Artwork

One significant factor contributing to the rise of NFTs in digital art is the ability to actualize 'digital collectors.' Because ownership of digital assets is programmatically verifiable via blockchain, it means collectors can own, display, and trade these assets with the same confidence that they would with physical assets.

This shift eliminates the need for a physical counterpart of the artwork, opening up new avenues for artists and enthusiasts to create, buy and sell digital art in formats that were previously difficult to monetize.

6.5. The Environmental Impact of NFTs

However, it's critical to look at other sides of the coin too. One significant drawback of NFTs is the environmental impact. The energy consumption of the Ethereum blockchain, which most NFTs are built on, relies primarily on fossil fuels and consumes a significant amount of power. This has led to serious concerns regarding the carbon footprint of NFT transactions.

6.6. Bridging into the Future

Looking past the hype and scrutiny, NFTs represent an interesting bridge between the physical and digital worlds. They offer artists a new medium for expression and a novel model for ownership. Their unique attributes make them a potentially attractive investment opportunity, yet they also illustrate how digital technologies continue to challenge current paradigms and open doors to uncharted territories.

Emerging trends within this space, such as fractional ownership of NFTs and the evolution of 'NFTfi' (NFT Finance) where NFTs are used as collateral in DeFi loans, pave the way towards a more inclusive and vibrant digital culture and economy.

In conclusion, NFTs and digital artworks represent a unique asset class that provide opportunities and challenges that are as diverse and complex as the digital world they exist within. It's a journey that has just begun, and the path to future will certainly be filled with twists, turns, and excitement.

Chapter 7. Digital Real Estate: Virtual Land Ownership and its Potential

As an investor in the digital age, you may have heard the term 'digital real estate' but may not be completely familiar with what it entails. This form of digital asset can be one of the most exciting and potentially lucrative in the world of online investing, rivalling physical real estate in its potential for returns.

7.1. Definition and Evolution of Digital Real Estate

Digital real estate, in its most basic form, refers to owning and controlling online space. Traditionally, this space took the form of domain names. Savvy investors would buy domain names hoping company owners would wish to purchase them in the future. Over time, this concept evolved to include more complex and valuable digital entities such as websites and blogs, which could generate ongoing passive income through advertising, affiliate marketing, and selling products and services.

Glancing back at the history of digital space, you will find the occurrence of some prodigious sales; For instance, Sex.com and Insurance.com domains, which were sold for around $13 million and $35.6 million, respectively. However, in recent years, a new form of digital real estate has emerged, transcending beyond the conceptual domain of webpages and blogs. This form—virtual land—exists within the metaverses of various games and virtual reality platforms.

7.2. Virtual Land and its Importance

Virtual land, just as physical land, can be bought, sold, developed, and rented out, all in exchange for real-world money. Although virtual, this land has real-world value and can generate substantial profits for its owners. The concept is similar to owning land in the physical world - scarce but desirable plots of virtual land can command a higher price. But, unlike physical land, virtual plots aren't bound by physical geography; their worth often stems from their coordinates within virtual worlds, their proximity to popular virtual locales, or their attached utilities.

One popular virtual world is Decentraland, a blockchain-based platform where users can purchase land through its native cryptocurrency, MANA. Remarkably, a piece of land in Decentraland was sold for 800,000 MANA, equivalent to roughly $200,000 in February 2020. The growing trend of such purchases isn't confined to Decentraland, as more and more VR platforms and games are selling their virtual land plots for hefty real-world prices.

7.3. Why Invest in Virtual Land?

Investing in virtual land comes with several potential benefits. Just like physical real estate investment, virtual counterparts offer opportunities to earn from appreciation, rent, and development.

With VR and augmented reality (AR) technologies maturing, the use of virtual space for entertainment, networking, and even professional uses is likely to increase. As the number of users in the virtual world grows, virtual land values can appreciate, yielding a return on the initial investment.

Additionally, owners can generate income by leasing or renting out their virtual properties. For example, they might rent their land to a business that wants to set up a virtual shop or to an individual who wants a 'home' location in the virtual world.

Furthermore, buying and developing virtual land can be cost-effective compared to physical land. Unlike physical properties, virtual plots do not require building materials or construction labor. Developers can erect virtual storefronts, houses, or event spaces at a fraction of the cost of their real-world counterparts, driving massive profit margins.

7.4. Risks of Virtual Land Investment

Just as there are potential upsides, investing in virtual land involves risks. No investment can guarantee returns, and virtual land is not different. The value of virtual land is volatile, tied to the popularity of the virtual world in which it resides, and can fluctuate wildly.

Moreover, the legal framework of virtual asset ownership is still evolving. In most countries, virtual assets are not recognized as legal properties, and hence, any disputes over ownership or usage rights could prove complex to resolve.

Additionally, the technology that supports and secures these virtual lands—usually Blockchain—while touted for its security, is not impervious to hacking or technical glitches. Such events could jeopardize the investment's security.

7.5. Steps to Invest in Virtual Land

While the process can vary slightly depending on the platform, here are the general steps to get started in virtual land investment.

1. Research Various Platforms: Just like researching neighborhoods before buying a physical property, you should study the various virtual worlds and their unique characteristics. Learn about their

user base, growth potential, and existing digital infrastructure.

2. Purchase Cryptocurrency: Most virtual land markets operate using specific cryptocurrencies. Familiarize yourself with crypto exchanges, wallets, and transactions.

3. Buy Land: Once you've chosen a platform and purchased the necessary cryptocurrency, you can buy land. Most platforms facilitate auctions for land sales.

4. Develop or Lease: After buying the land, you can choose to develop it by constructing buildings or creating experiences or lease it out for others to use.

5. Keep Up with the Market: Stay abreast of the latest developments, as the value of your land could fluctuate with the popularity of the game or platform it's in.

In conclusion, digital real estate, particularly virtual land, presents an exciting investment opportunity as technology and digital trends continue to evolve. While it calls for savvy investing, knowledge about cryptocurrencies, and an understanding of the virtual worlds, returns can be significant. However, it's important to carefully consider the risks involved. As with any investment, thorough knowledge and research are key to success.

Chapter 8. The Mechanics of Decentralized Finance (DeFi)

In the thrilling world of digital assets, one sector has shown significant promise; its transformative potential is just beginning to be understood. That sector is Decentralized Finance, or DeFi.

DeFi is an experimental, rapidly evolving sector of the digital economy leveraging blockchain technologies to disrupt traditional financial systems. It establishes financial products in a decentralized architecture outside of companies' and governments' control, dramatically expanding the borders of financial inclusion.

8.1. Understanding DeFi

DeFI offers a complete ecosystem of financial instruments and services, such as savings and checking accounts, loans, asset trading, insurance, and more, universally accessible using blockchain technology. The entire ecosystem is operated by smart contracts, autonomous computer code executing on the blockchain.

Smart contracts are protocols automatically enforcing the contract's rules and transferring digital assets. They eliminate the need for trusted intermediaries in financial transactions, resulting in a fast, efficient, and affordable financial system that truly runs 24/7.

Blockchain's decentralization, transparency, and high security underlie these operations. Nearly every action on the blockchain is completely transparent and can be audited by any participant. Yet, the participants themselves can remain pseudonymous, providing a unique blend of accountability and privacy.

8.2. Instruments of DeFi

The heart of DeFi lies in its financial instruments. Designed to mimic traditional financial instruments, these use blockchain technology to create superior, more inclusive counterparts.

- DEXs (Decentralized Exchanges) let users trade digital assets directly, without any intermediaries. DEXs use automated market makers and liquidity pools rather than order books to set prices and facilitate trades, offering deep liquidity and minimal slippage.

- Lending platforms loan digital assets through liquidity pools, with interest rates determined algorithmically based on supply and demand.

- Stablecoins are digital assets pegged to a stable asset like gold or fiat currency, helping to manage volatility in the cryptocurrency market. Examples include USD Coin (USDC) and DAI.

- Yield farming or liquidity mining allows cryptoholders to earn rewards for providing liquidity in DeFi markets. The lenders earn yields based on several factors, including liquidity pool interest, platform token rewards and fees from trades.

- Insurance protocols provide coverage against smart contract failures or other risks in the DeFi environment. Examples include Nexus Mutual and Cover Protocol.

8.3. Participating in DeFi

DeFi runs on public blockchains. While Ethereum is currently the most popular because its smart contract capabilities lay an ideal ground for DeFi, networks like Binance Smart Chain, Polkadot, and Solana are emerging as strong competitors.

Any DeFi tool can be accessed by setting up a digital wallet, such as

Metamask or WalletConnect, and then connecting it to the blockchain. Wallets store your digital assets and your private keys, which are essentially your password to interact with the blockchains. Security with digital wallets is of utmost importance, as losing your private keys is akin to losing your assets.

To participate in DeFi, you first need access to cryptocurrency, often Ether (ETH) or a network-specific token. From there, you can engage with DeFi platforms to trade assets, provide liquidity, borrow, lend, stake, farm yields, and more.

8.4. Lessons from Financial History

The DeFi journey isn't without risk. Flash loan attacks, smart contract bugs, and systemic failures are all risks inherent to the DeFi landscape. These echo the financial challenges faced by traditional finance institutions through history. Banks, for example, were not built in a day nor without trials. It is essential to understand that the DeFi space is still maturing and susceptible to anomalies and risks.

However, the DeFi proponents' promise is a fully decentralized financial system that is accessible to all and able to provide more efficient and inclusive financial services, giving new shapes to our economies. The allure of DeFi lies in the unification of finance and technology, enabling the decoupling of economic progress from traditional centralized systems.

8.5. DeFi and the Future of Finance

Despite the risks, DeFi's impact is undeniably growing. Its principles of openness, transparency, and inclusivity align well with a digital-native generation looking beyond traditional financial systems. Through DeFi, personal finance is becoming truly personal, and financial sovereignty is within reach.

The key to unlocking success in DeFi is knowledge. Understanding technology and economics behind DeFi, keeping an eye on the broader blockchain space, and always staying informed will help you navigate this bold new frontier of finance.

In the future, decentralized finance could become a standard, either replacing traditional financial systems or helping them evolve into something better. The journey of understanding DeFi, therefore, is an investment in the future – a future that is rapidly coming towards us. As our economies advance, what was once complex and reserved for a few might be standard knowledge for all – a testament to the evolution of society in this digital age. Understanding DeFi is the first step in witnessing this evolution. Stand ready to embrace the future of finance, today.

Chapter 9. Blockchain Technology: The Backbone of Digital Assets

Understanding blockchain technology is crucial to fully appreciating the innovative potential of digital assets. Concrete in structure, yet flexible by design, blockchain has been the watermark for a myriad of advancements in the field of online investing and assets creation.

9.1. The Basics of Blockchain

In simple terms, blockchain is a form of distributed ledger technology (DLT). It is essentially a chain of blocks, where each block contains a list of transactions. These transactions are verified by a swarm of computers—called nodes—spread across the world, making the system decentralised.

Each block is linked to its predecessor through a cryptographic hash function. This linking mechanism ensures that once a block is added to the chain, it becomes practically immutable. Imagine a series of storage boxes, where each box is secured to the previous one through a complex mathematical lock. If one were to try altering the content inside a box, the locks securing that box and all subsequent boxes would instantly break, alerting the entire system to the interference.

This essential structure is one of the reasons the blockchain's security is highly regarded. It provides transparency and trust in a system where trust is not given to a single authority but distributed among peers.

9.2. How Does Blockchain Work?

Technically, a blockchain works through a consensus mechanism. A new transaction, once initiated, is broadcasted to all nodes. These nodes, or miners in the case of Bitcoin, use their computational power to solve a complex mathematical problem. The one who solves it first gets to add the block of transactions to the chain and is rewarded for their effort.

This process is often called 'Proof of Work', which assures that no single node can monopolize the addition of blocks. It is this concept that distributed control among the nodes and eliminates the need for a central regulating authority.

Once added, a block and its transactions are there for all to see and verify. The transparency of blockchain becomes its strength - no one can dispute a transaction, and every participant can independently track the transactions occurring in the system.

9.3. Potential and Scope

The potential of blockchain technology extends far beyond cryptocurrencies like Bitcoin and Ethereum. Digital assets such as non-fungible tokens (NFTs), decentralized finance (DeFi) applications, and smart contracts have all been enabled by blockchain's unique properties.

In the realm of digital art, NFTs have created an entirely new asset class that assigns value to unique, irreproducible digital items. And in finance, DeFi applications have begun to provide block-chain-mediated financial services without the need for intermediaries.

Smart contracts — self-executing contracts with terms and conditions directly written into code — have further broadened the possibilities of blockchain. These digital agreements execute automatically once certain conditions are met, eliminating the need for intermediaries such as brokers or lawyers.

Such advancements are transforming industries and creating opportunities for investors and developers alike. By understanding the technology behind these developments, one can better appraise the potential and risks associated with digital assets.

9.4. The Challenge and Promise Ahead

Blockchain technology, despite its potential, comes with a set of challenges. Scalability issues, energy consumption, and regulatory uncertainties stand as barriers obstructing its mainstream adoption.

Proof of work, the consensus algorithm used by many blockchains, is infamous for its substantial energy consumption. As blockchain networks grow in size and complexity, they're likely to face bottlenecks that can slow down transactions and escalate costs.

Simultaneously, regulatory uncertainty surrounding decentralized technology poses a significant hurdle. Regulations are often lagging behind the pace of innovation, which leads to legal ambiguities and instigates risk and volatility.

Nevertheless, with multitudes of creative minds working to overcome these challenges, the promise of blockchain technology far outweighs its difficulties. Whether in providing a reliable means of value storage or catalyzing the creation of novel asset classes, blockchain technology stands firm at the core of the digital asset revolution.

By embracing the intricacies of this cutting-edge technology, you are better equipped to appreciate the myriad of opportunities presented by digital assets, and poised to navigate the fascinating world of web-based wealth creation with newfound insight and understanding. As the digital asset landscape continues to evolve, those equipped with knowledge will be in a prime position to ride the wave of this innovative and rapidly changing frontier.

Chapter 10. Risk Management in the Digital Asset Space

As we set foot into the dynamic realm of digital assets, one term that frequently comes to the fore is "Risk Management". Spanning a range of hazards, from the volatility of cryptocurrency markets to cybersecurity threats, managing such risks becomes imperative for anyone participating in this space.

10.1. The Fundamental Principles of Risk Management

Before delving deeper into specific risk management strategies for digital assets, it's essential to understand the underpinnings of risk management at large. Risk management embodies an organized and systematic approach to identifying, evaluating, and controlling or mitigating potential threats or uncertain events that could adversely affect the objectives and operations of an investment.

The rudimentary and universally acknowledged principles of risk management comprise:

- Identifying risk: Ascertain what could threaten the achievement of the targets.

- Evaluating risk: Quantify the potential impact of a risk, accounting for both its probability and potential damages.

- Mitigating risk: Based on risk evaluations, devise action plans to tackle these possible threats.

These principles set the guidelines for managing risks associated with digital assets.

10.2. Understanding Types of Risks in the Digital Asset Space

Digital assets present risks that are both similar to traditional investments and distinctively unique. A comprehensive risk management strategy must account for all possible risk types.

1. Market Risk: This refers to the risk of financial loss from adverse market movements such as price fluctuation, which is a trademark of digital assets. Cryptocurrencies like Bitcoin have proven highly volatile, and this inconsistent price trajectory presents substantial market risk.

2. Liquidity Risk: Some digital assets may have low liquidity or a small trading volume, increasing the chances of slippage and hindering the ability to buy or sell assets swiftly without affecting the market price significantly.

3. Operational Risk: Like any other business operation, digital asset management brings operational risks, including system failures, malfunctions, human errors, and process inefficiencies.

4. Regulatory Risk: As the digital asset space is still nascent, regulatory frameworks are rapidly evolving; changes can dramatically impact asset prices and legality.

5. Security Risk: This encompasses the risk of hack attacks and unauthorized access leading to asset theft or loss. The irreversible nature of blockchain transactions exacerbates this risk.

6. Legal and Reputational Risks: For assets involved in illicit activities, there's a risk of damaging reputations and facing legal consequences.

10.3. Risk Mitigation Strategies for Digital Assets

1. Diversification: Much like traditional investing, one of the best risk management tactics in the digital asset space is diversification. Spreading investments across a range of digital assets can mitigate the impact of a single asset's poor performance.

2. Due Diligence: Conduct thorough research before investing, including checking the credibility of the digital asset, the team behind it, the problem it claims to solve, and its technology.

3. Professional Guidance: A professional financial advisor with digital asset sector experience can guide the investment journey, helping investors make informed decisions.

4. Security: Cybersecurity practices are a must in the digital asset environment – use encrypted wallets, two-factor authentication, and other advanced security protocols.

5. Regulatory compliance: Stay up to date with local and global regulations pertaining to digital assets to help manage regulatory risk.

6. Insurance: Some digital asset exchanges provide insurance – this can mitigate potential losses from theft or hacks on the exchange.

7. Set Stop Losses/Limits: For cryptocurrencies and other similar digital assets, setting stop losses is critical to cap potential losses.

10.4. Technological Developments in Risk Management

Worthy of note is the role of technology in bolstering risk management for digital assets. A slew of fintech innovations is simplifying the process of identifying, evaluating, and mitigating risks in this space.

- Blockchain Auditing Tools: Used to detect anomalous transactions that might indicate fraudulent activity or asset theft.

- Predictive Analytics: Leveraging AI and machine learning can provide insights and predictions on market trends, helping manage market risk.

- Cybersecurity tech: Advanced security solutions up the ante in protecting digital assets.

10.5. Conclusion: A Balancing Act

Risk management in digital asset investing is a delicate balance. It requires taking calculated risks to maximize returns while putting in place robust measures that insulate against potential negative impacts. By understanding and following the principles of risk management mapped out and harnessing technological tools, investors can navigate the choppy waters of digital assets with firm confidence.

Despite its challenges, the digital asset space remains ripe with potential. Therefore, effective risk management remains a cardinal rule for anyone hoping to realize significant returns in the sector. With the right strategies, any participating individual or institution stands to gain deeply from the revolution that digital assets represent.

In a landscape as dynamic and high-stake as digital assets, risk management isn't a choice – it's an individual and collective necessity that we must nurture and uphold for the sake of our digital future.

Chapter 11. Succeeding in Digital Investment: Practical Tips and Strategies

Investing in digital assets can be a game-changing venture, introducing opportunities for substantial returns and paving a path toward financial independence. The key to successive digital investing lies in understanding the nuances of the digital market and the application of practical strategies to mitigate potential risks.

11.1. Understanding the Digital Investment Landscape

The digital investment domain encompasses a wide array of asset types, ranging from cryptocurrencies like Bitcoin and Ethereum, to digital stocks, bonds, and equities, and other blockchain-based tokens such as Non-Fungible Tokens (NFTs).

We have witnessed the rise and fall of numerous digital assets, hinged on a multitude of factors - evolving technology, market supply and demand, regulatory constraints, global socio-economic trends, and more. Therefore, fully comprehending the digital investment landscape is crucial if you wish to thrive in it.

11.2. Stay Informed

Staying informed is not merely a tip but a requirement in the digital investment world. Each day brings forth new developments, whether they're technological advancements, regulatory changes, or market trends.

Investors should regularly read reliable financial news sources, join online investment forums, subscribe to industry newsletters, watch educational content, and engage with thought leaders and experts on social media platforms. Continuous learning will not only keep you updated but also provide you with a multi-faceted understanding of the market, empowering you to make informed decisions.

11.3. Diversify Your Digital Investment

A common investment mantra "Don't put all your eggs in one basket" rings true even in the digital world. Diversifying your digital investment portfolio spreads the risk across different assets, sectors, and geographical locations.

While each segment of the digital environment operates distinctly, they often interact and influence each other. For instance, fluctuations in cryptocurrency prices may impact blockchain technology stocks or vice versa. Diversification allows investors to capitalize on these interconnections, balancing potential losses in one asset with gains in another.

11.4. Risk Management

While digital investments offer significant potential for high returns, they are also highly volatile and subject to potential losses resulting from market fluctuations and technological changes. As a digital investor, risk management should be at the heart of your strategy.

Invest only what you can afford to lose, avoid impulsive decisions, remain patient during market shifts, and consider your long-term goals. Implementing risk management tools, like stop-loss orders or diversification, can also help curb potential losses.

11.5. Integrate Technology for Better Decision-Making

In the era of digital investments, many advanced analytical tools have been designed to aid investors in decision-making. Such tools leverage artificial intelligence, machine learning, and big data analytics to provide in-depth market analyses, predictive modeling, automated trading, portfolio management, and risk assessment.

These technologies can be utilized by anyone, regardless of their technical expertise. Choosing the right tech support based on your needs can greatly augment your investment strategy, leading to more efficient and profitable decision-making.

11.6. Regulation and Compliance

The digital investment landscape is continually evolving, and so is its regulatory framework. Investors must familiarize themselves with the laws and regulations pertaining to digital asset investment in their respective countries.

Compliance is critical not only to avoid legal repercussions but also to maintain the integrity and security of your investments. Regulatory changes can significantly impact the performance of your digital assets, indicating the importance of staying updated on the regulatory environment.

11.7. Planning for the Long Term

Short-term fluctuations in the digital market can be unnerving for investors, especially beginners. It is essential to keep in mind that investing, especially in the digital realm, should ideally be viewed as a long-term endeavor.

Consistently monitoring your investments and adjusting your strategy based on market trends and personal financial goals can yield sustainable profits in the long run. Remember, patience and persistence are vital in the digital investment world.

Digital investment is a vast and dynamic field. With the right knowledge, strategies, and tools, you can navigate its intricacies and reap substantial benefits. Stay informed, diversify, manage risks, integrate technology, comply with regulations and plan for the long term - the key components of a successful digital investment journey.

www.ingramcontent.com/pod-product-compliance
Lightning Source LLC
LaVergne TN
LVHW051626050326
832903LV00033B/4676